A Chocolate Moose

for Dinner

written and illustrated by
FRED GWYNNE

Windmill/Wanderer Books

New York

First published in the United States in 1976.
This edition published by WINDMILL BOOKS, Inc. and
WANDERER BOOKS, a Simon & Schuster Division of Gulf & Western Corporation.
All rights reserved under International
and Pan-American Copyright Conventions.
Simon & Schuster Building
1230 Avenue of the Americas
New York, New York 10020
WINDMILL BOOKS and colophon are trademarks of Windmill Books, Inc.
registered in the United States Patent and Trademark Office.
WANDERER is a trademark of Simon & Schuster.
Designed by Dorothea von Elbe
Printed and bound in Hong Kong by Dai Nippon Printing Co., (Hong Kong) Ltd.

Library of Congress Cataloging in Publication Data

Gwynne, Fred.
   A chocolate moose for dinner.

   SUMMARY: A little girl pictures the things her
parents talk about, such as a chocolate moose,
a gorilla war, and shoe trees.
   1. English language—Homonyms—Juvenile
literature.   [1. English language—Homonyms.
2. English language—Terms and phrases]   I. Title.
PE1595.G73   1980   428.1   80-14150
ISBN 0-671-96209-4
ISBN 0-671-96094-6 (pbk.)

For Keiron, Gaynor, Madyn, Evan, and Furlaud

**Mommy says
she had a
chocolate moose
for dinner last night.**

And after dinner

she toasted Daddy.

there's a gorilla war.

Daddy says
he has trees
for all his shoes.

Daddy says
lions pray on

other animals.

Daddy says he hates

the arms race.

Mommy says we need a new wing on the house, but Daddy says he'll have to sleep on it.

Daddy says there should

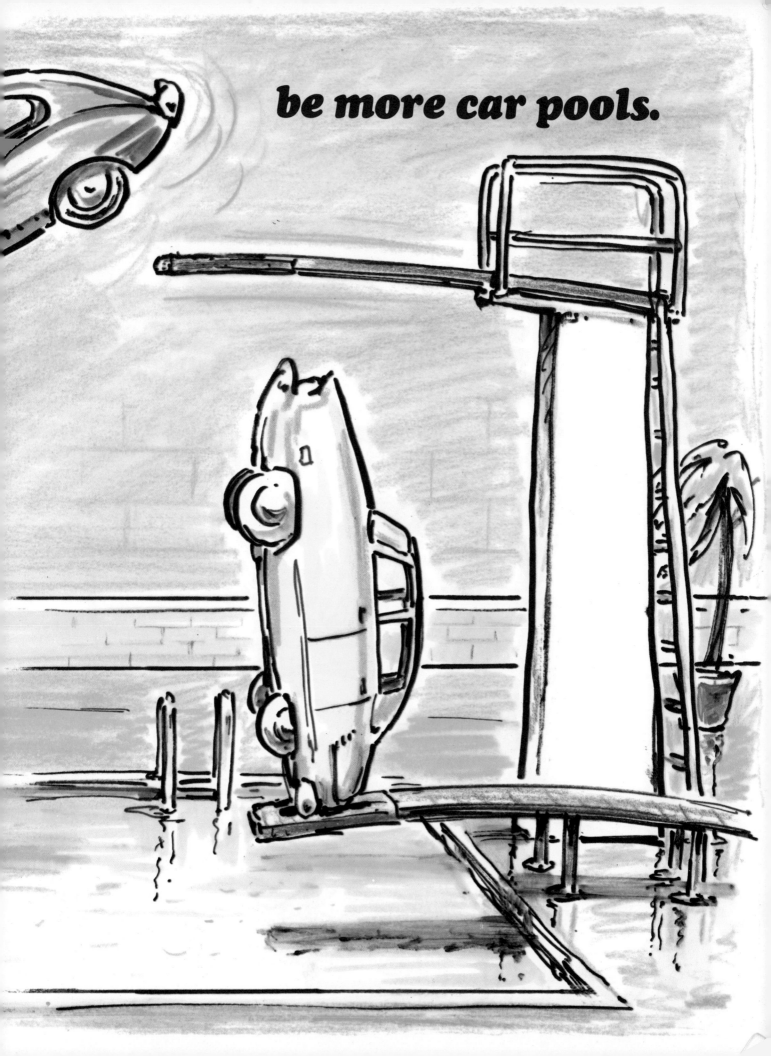

Mommy says her

favorite painter is Dolly.

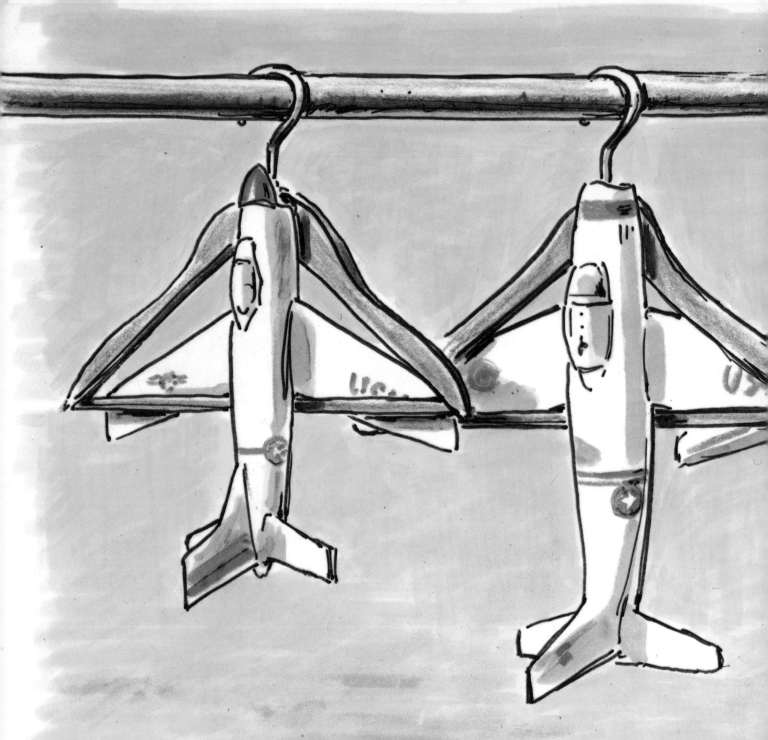

Mommy says there are airplane hangers.

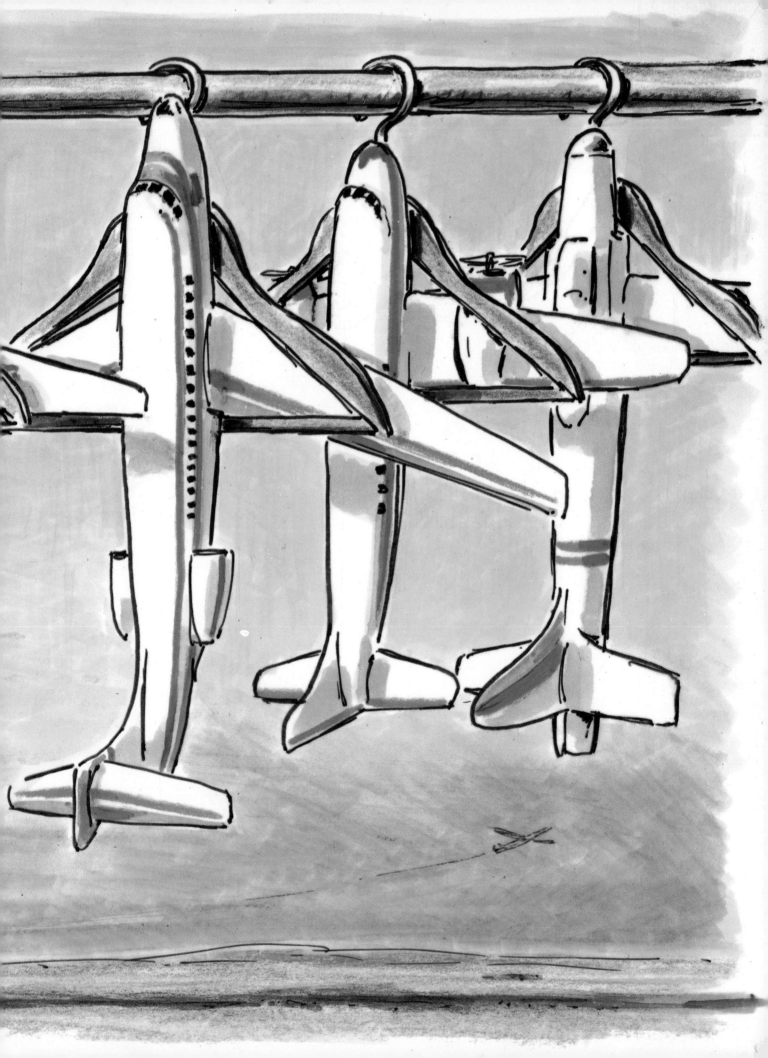

**Daddy says
he has the best
fishing tackle.**

It says on TV a man held up a bank.

He spent two years
in the pen.

And he has just escaped and is now on the lamb.

At the ocean Daddy says

Daddy says he plays the piano by ear.

Daddy says that in college

people row in shells.

**And some row
in a single skull.**

Mommy says after she and Daddy argue they always kiss and make up.

**Mommy says
she's going to tell me
about Santa Claws.**

And Daddy says he's going to tell me the story of

the tortoise and the hair.

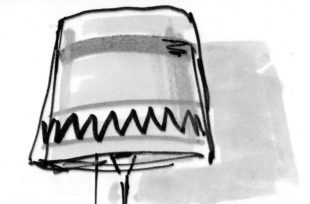

**Stories
like these
drive me
up a wall!**